HOCKEY
Journal

NAME _____

SEASON YEAR _____

TEAM NAME _____

My Hockey Journal

©The Life Graduate Publishing Group

No part of this book may be scanned, reproduced or distributed in any printed or electronic form without the prior permission of the author or publisher.

My Hockey Journal

-Hockey-

My Hockey Journal

-Hockey-

HOCKEY Journal SECTIONS

01 Season Goals
Write down your Top 3 Season Goals

02 Training & Game Logbook
Record your training sessions and game details

03 Season Notes
Write further details of your season to keep a record for future reference

04 Autographs & Photos
Gather the autographs and photos of team members, coaches and famous players

01

SEASON GOALS

01 HOCKEY SEASON GOALS

GOAL 1 ....

GOAL 2 ....

GOAL 3 ....

My Hockey Journal

-Hockey-

02
TRAINING & GAME LOGBOOK

TRAINING

Date: / /

Start time :

End time :

Skills Completed
Write down the skills you worked on and developed during your training sessions

....
....
....
....

Skills to improve
Write down areas that you can improve on for your next training session

....
....
....
....

Coach & Team Focus
Write down if your coach or team has a skill or game focus you are working on

....
....

Extra Notes
Do you have additional notes or thoughts you would like to write down?

....
....
....

GAME DAY

Date: /   /   **Start time**   :

Location: ....

Home Game ○   **Away Game** ○

Game Details

.... **Vs** ....

Game Result

           Goals   Goals

Our Score   Opposition Score

Coach Feedback

....
....
....

My Performance
Write down how you felt you contributed to the game. Did the coach provide you any personal feedback? Did you have any highlights? Did you have areas of improvement?

....
....
....
....
....
....

TRAINING

Date: / /   **Start time** :

End time :

Skills Completed Write down the skills you worked on and developed during your training sessions

....
....
....
....

Skills to improve Write down areas that you can improve on for your next training session

....
....
....
....

Coach & Team Focus Write down if your coach or team has a skill or game focus you are working on

....
....

Extra Notes Do you have additional notes or thoughts you would like to write down?

....
....
....

GAME DAY

Date: / /   **Start time** :

Location: ....

Home Game ◯   **Away Game** ◯

Game Details

.... **Vs** ....

Game Result

        Goals   Goals

Our Score   Opposition Score

Coach Feedback

....
....
....

My Performance

Write down how you felt you contributed to the game. Did the coach provide you any personal feedback? Did you have any highlights? Did you have areas of improvement?

....
....
....
....
....

TRAINING

Date: / /

Start time :

End time :

Skills Completed
Write down the skills you worked on and developed during your training sessions

....
....
....
....

Skills to improve
Write down areas that you can improve on for your next training session

....
....
....
....

Coach & Team Focus
Write down if your coach or team has a skill or game focus you are working on

....
....

Extra Notes
Do you have additional notes or thoughts you would like to write down?

....
....
....

GAME DAY

Date: /   /   **Start time**   :

Location: ....

Home Game ○   **Away Game** ○

Game Details

.... **Vs** ....

Game Result

        Goals   Goals

Our Score   Opposition Score

Coach Feedback

....
....
....

My Performance

Write down how you felt you contributed to the game. Did the coach provide you any personal feedback? Did you have any highlights? Did you have areas of improvement?

....
....
....
....
....
....

TRAINING

Date: / / **Start time** :

End time :

Skills Completed Write down the skills you worked on and developed during your training sessions

....
....
....
....

Skills to improve Write down areas that you can improve on for your next training session

....
....
....
....

Coach & Team Focus Write down if your coach or team has a skill or game focus you are working on

....
....

Extra Notes Do you have additional notes or thoughts you would like to write down?

....
....
....

GAME DAY

Date: / /   **Start time** :

Location: ....

Home Game   **Away Game**

Game Details

.... **Vs** ....

Game Result

　　　　Goals　　　　　　　　　　　Goals

Our Score　　　　　Opposition Score

Coach Feedback

....
....
....

My Performance   Write down how you felt you contributed to the game. Did the coach provide you any personal feedback? Did you have any highlights? Did you have areas of improvement?

....
....
....
....
....

TRAINING

Date: / /   **Start time** :

End time :

Skills Completed Write down the skills you worked on and developed during your training sessions

....
....
....
....

Skills to improve Write down areas that you can improve on for your next training session

....
....
....
....

Coach & Team Focus Write down if your coach or team has a skill or game focus you are working on

....
....

Extra Notes Do you have additional notes or thoughts you would like to write down?

....
....
....

GAME DAY

Date: /   /   **Start time**   :

Location: ....

Home Game ○   **Away Game** ○

Game Details

.... **Vs** ....

Game Result

　　　　　Goals　　　　　　　　　　　　Goals

Our Score　　　　　　Opposition Score

Coach Feedback

....
....
....

My Performance   Write down how you felt you contributed to the game. Did the coach provide you any personal feedback? Did you have any highlights? Did you have areas of improvement?

....
....
....
....
....
....

TRAINING

Date: / / **Start time** :

End time :

Skills Completed   Write down the skills you worked on and developed during your training sessions

....
....
....
....

Skills to improve   Write down areas that you can improve on for your next training session

....
....
....
....

Coach & Team Focus   Write down if your coach or team has a skill or game focus you are working on

....
....

Extra Notes   Do you have additional notes or thoughts you would like to write down?

....
....
....

GAME DAY

Date: /   /   **Start time**   :

Location: ....

Home Game ⬤   **Away Game** ⬤

Game Details

.... **Vs** ....

Game Result

               Goals   Goals

Our Score   Opposition Score

Coach Feedback

....
....
....

My Performance

Write down how you felt you contributed to the game. Did the coach provide you any personal feedback? Did you have any highlights? Did you have areas of improvement?

....
....
....
....
....

TRAINING

Date: / / **Start time** :

End time :

Skills Completed
Write down the skills you worked on and developed during your training sessions

....
....
....
....

Skills to improve
Write down areas that you can improve on for your next training session

....
....
....
....

Coach & Team Focus
Write down if your coach or team has a skill or game focus you are working on

....
....

Extra Notes
Do you have additional notes or thoughts you would like to write down?

....
....
....

GAME DAY

Date: /   /   **Start time**   :

Location: ....

Home Game ●   **Away Game** ●

Game Details

.... **Vs** ....

Game Result

          Goals   Goals

Our Score   Opposition Score

Coach Feedback

....
....
....

My Performance   Write down how you felt you contributed to the game. Did the coach provide you any personal feedback? Did you have any highlights? Did you have areas of improvement?

....
....
....
....
....
....

TRAINING

Date: / / **Start time** :

End time :

Skills Completed
Write down the skills you worked on and developed during your training sessions

....
....
....
....

Skills to improve
Write down areas that you can improve on for your next training session

....
....
....
....

Coach & Team Focus
Write down if your coach or team has a skill or game focus you are working on

....
....

Extra Notes
Do you have additional notes or thoughts you would like to write down?

....
....
....

GAME DAY

Date: / /   **Start time**   :

Location: ....

Home Game ○   **Away Game** ○

Game Details

.... **Vs** ....

Game Result

         Goals   Goals

Our Score   Opposition Score

Coach Feedback

....
....
....

My Performance   Write down how you felt you contributed to the game. Did the coach provide you any personal feedback? Did you have any highlights? Did you have areas of improvement?

....
....
....
....
....

TRAINING

Date: / /

Start time :

End time :

Skills Completed
Write down the skills you worked on and developed during your training sessions

....
....
....
....

Skills to improve
Write down areas that you can improve on for your next training session

....
....
....
....

Coach & Team Focus
Write down if your coach or team has a skill or game focus you are working on

....
....

Extra Notes
Do you have additional notes or thoughts you would like to write down?

....
....
....

GAME DAY

Date: / /   **Start time**   :

Location: ....

Home Game ○   **Away Game** ○

Game Details

.... **Vs** ....

Game Result

        Goals   Goals

Our Score   Opposition Score

Coach Feedback

....
....
....

My Performance
Write down how you felt you contributed to the game. Did the coach provide you any personal feedback? Did you have any highlights? Did you have areas of improvement?

....
....
....
....
....
....

TRAINING

Date: / /

Start time :

End time :

Skills Completed
Write down the skills you worked on and developed during your training sessions

....
....
....
....

Skills to improve
Write down areas that you can improve on for your next training session

....
....
....
....

Coach & Team Focus
Write down if your coach or team has a skill or game focus you are working on

....
....

Extra Notes
Do you have additional notes or thoughts you would like to write down?

....
....
....

GAME DAY

Date: / /   **Start time**   :

Location: ....

Home Game   **Away Game**

Game Details

.... **Vs** ....

Game Result

.... Goals   .... Goals

Our Score   Opposition Score

Coach Feedback

....
....
....

My Performance
Write down how you felt you contributed to the game. Did the coach provide you any personal feedback? Did you have any highlights? Did you have areas of improvement?

....
....
....
....
....

TRAINING

Date: / / **Start time** :

 End time :

Skills Completed   Write down the skills you worked on and developed during your training sessions

....
....
....
....

Skills to improve   Write down areas that you can improve on for your next training session

....
....
....
....

Coach & Team Focus   Write down if your coach or team has a skill or game focus you are working on

....
....

Extra Notes   Do you have additional notes or thoughts you would like to write down?

....
....
....

GAME DAY

Date: / /   **Start time**   :

Location: ....

Home Game ⚪   **Away Game** ⚪

Game Details

.... **Vs** ....

Game Result

        Goals   Goals

Our Score   Opposition Score

Coach Feedback

....
....
....

My Performance   Write down how you felt you contributed to the game. Did the coach provide you any personal feedback? Did you have any highlights? Did you have areas of improvement?

....
....
....
....
....

TRAINING

Date: / / **Start time** :
 End time :

Skills Completed   Write down the skills you worked on and developed during your training sessions

....
....
....
....

Skills to improve   Write down areas that you can improve on for your next training session

....
....
....
....

Coach & Team Focus   Write down if your coach or team has a skill or game focus you are working on

....
....

Extra Notes   Do you have additional notes or thoughts you would like to write down?

....
....
....

GAME DAY

Date: / /   **Start time**   :

Location: ....

Home Game ⚪   **Away Game** ⚪

Game Details

.... **Vs** ....

Game Result

      Goals   Goals

Our Score   Opposition Score

Coach Feedback

....
....
....

My Performance   Write down how you felt you contributed to the game. Did the coach provide you any personal feedback? Did you have any highlights? Did you have areas of improvement?

....
....
....
....
....

TRAINING

Date: / /

Start time :

End time :

Skills Completed
Write down the skills you worked on and developed during your training sessions

....
....
....
....

Skills to improve
Write down areas that you can improve on for your next training session

....
....
....
....

Coach & Team Focus
Write down if your coach or team has a skill or game focus you are working on

....
....

Extra Notes
Do you have additional notes or thoughts you would like to write down?

....
....
....

GAME DAY

Date: / /   **Start time** :

Location: ....

Home Game ⬤   **Away Game** ⬤

Game Details

.... **Vs** ....

Game Result

         Goals   Goals

Our Score   Opposition Score

Coach Feedback

....
....
....

My Performance — Write down how you felt you contributed to the game. Did the coach provide you any personal feedback? Did you have any highlights? Did you have areas of improvement?

....
....
....
....
....

TRAINING

Date: / / **Start time** :

End time :

Skills Completed Write down the skills you worked on and developed during your training sessions

....
....
....
....

Skills to improve Write down areas that you can improve on for your next training session

....
....
....
....

Coach & Team Focus Write down if your coach or team has a skill or game focus you are working on

....
....

Extra Notes Do you have additional notes or thoughts you would like to write down?

....
....
....

GAME DAY

Date: /   /   **Start time**   :

Location: ....

Home Game ⚪   **Away Game** ⚪

Game Details

.... **Vs** ....

Game Result

          Goals   Goals

Our Score   Opposition Score

Coach Feedback

....
....
....

My Performance   Write down how you felt you contributed to the game. Did the coach provide you any personal feedback? Did you have any highlights? Did you have areas of improvement?

....
....
....
....
....

TRAINING

Date: / /

Start time :

End time :

Skills Completed
Write down the skills you worked on and developed during your training sessions

....
....
....
....

Skills to improve
Write down areas that you can improve on for your next training session

....
....
....
....

Coach & Team Focus
Write down if your coach or team has a skill or game focus you are working on

....
....

Extra Notes
Do you have additional notes or thoughts you would like to write down?

....
....
....

GAME DAY

Date: / /   **Start time** :

Location: ....

Home Game ○   **Away Game** ○

Game Details

.... **Vs** ....

Game Result

　　　　　Goals　　　　　　　　　　　　Goals

Our Score　　　　　　Opposition Score

Coach Feedback

....
....
....

My Performance   Write down how you felt you contributed to the game. Did the coach provide you any personal feedback? Did you have any highlights? Did you have areas of improvement?

....
....
....
....
....
....

TRAINING

Date: / /

Start time :

End time :

Skills Completed Write down the skills you worked on and developed during your training sessions

....
....
....
....

Skills to improve Write down areas that you can improve on for your next training session

....
....
....
....

Coach & Team Focus Write down if your coach or team has a skill or game focus you are working on

....
....

Extra Notes Do you have additional notes or thoughts you would like to write down?

....
....
....

GAME DAY

Date: /   /   **Start time**   :

Location: ....

Home Game ⚪   **Away Game** ⚪

Game Details

.... **Vs** ....

Game Result

           Goals   Goals

Our Score   Opposition Score

Coach Feedback

....
....
....

My Performance Write down how you felt you contributed to the game. Did the coach provide you any personal feedback? Did you have any highlights? Did you have areas of improvement?

....
....
....
....
....

TRAINING

Date: / / **Start time** :

End time :

Skills Completed
Write down the skills you worked on and developed during your training sessions

....
....
....
....

Skills to improve
Write down areas that you can improve on for your next training session

....
....
....
....

Coach & Team Focus
Write down if your coach or team has a skill or game focus you are working on

....
....

Extra Notes
Do you have additional notes or thoughts you would like to write down?

....
....
....

GAME DAY

Date: /   /   **Start time**   :

Location: ....

Home Game ⚪   **Away Game** ⚪

Game Details

.... **Vs** ....

Game Result

            Goals   Goals

Our Score   Opposition Score

Coach Feedback

....
....
....

My Performance
Write down how you felt you contributed to the game. Did the coach provide you any personal feedback? Did you have any highlights? Did you have areas of improvement?

....
....
....
....
....

TRAINING

Date: / /

Start time :

End time :

Skills Completed   Write down the skills you worked on and developed during your training sessions

....
....
....
....

Skills to improve   Write down areas that you can improve on for your next training session

....
....
....
....

Coach & Team Focus   Write down if your coach or team has a skill or game focus you are working on

....
....

Extra Notes   Do you have additional notes or thoughts you would like to write down?

....
....
....

GAME DAY

Date: /   /   **Start time**   :

Location: ....

Home Game ⬤   **Away Game** ⬤

Game Details

.... **Vs** ....

Game Result

            Goals   Goals

Our Score   Opposition Score

Coach Feedback

....
....
....

My Performance   Write down how you felt you contributed to the game. Did the coach provide you any personal feedback? Did you have any highlights? Did you have areas of improvement?

....
....
....
....
....

TRAINING

Date: / / **Start time** :

End time :

Skills Completed
Write down the skills you worked on and developed during your training sessions

....
....
....
....

Skills to improve
Write down areas that you can improve on for your next training session

....
....
....
....

Coach & Team Focus
Write down if your coach or team has a skill or game focus you are working on

....
....

Extra Notes
Do you have additional notes or thoughts you would like to write down?

....
....
....

GAME DAY

Date: / /   **Start time** :

Location: ....

Home Game   **Away Game**

Game Details

.... **Vs** ....

Game Result

　　　　Goals　　　　　　　　　　　Goals

Our Score　　　　　Opposition Score

Coach Feedback

....
....
....

My Performance   Write down how you felt you contributed to the game. Did the coach provide you any personal feedback? Did you have any highlights? Did you have areas of improvement?

....
....
....
....
....

TRAINING

Date: / /   **Start time** :

End time :

Skills Completed   Write down the skills you worked on and developed during your training sessions

....
....
....
....

Skills to improve   Write down areas that you can improve on for your next training session

....
....
....
....

Coach & Team Focus   Write down if your coach or team has a skill or game focus you are working on

....
....

Extra Notes   Do you have additional notes or thoughts you would like to write down?

....
....
....

GAME DAY

Date: / /   **Start time** :

Location: ....

Home Game   **Away Game**

Game Details

.... **Vs** ....

Game Result

        Goals   Goals

Our Score   Opposition Score

Coach Feedback

....
....
....

My Performance   Write down how you felt you contributed to the game. Did the coach provide you any personal feedback? Did you have any highlights? Did you have areas of improvement?

....
....
....
....
....

TRAINING

Date: / /   **Start time** :

End time :

Skills Completed   Write down the skills you worked on and developed during your training sessions

....
....
....
....

Skills to improve   Write down areas that you can improve on for your next training session

....
....
....
....

Coach & Team Focus   Write down if your coach or team has a skill or game focus you are working on

....
....

Extra Notes   Do you have additional notes or thoughts you would like to write down?

....
....
....

GAME DAY

Date: /   /   **Start time**   :

Location: ....

Home Game ⬤   **Away Game** ⬤

Game Details

.... **Vs** ....

Game Result

         Goals   Goals

Our Score   Opposition Score

Coach Feedback

....
....
....

My Performance

Write down how you felt you contributed to the game. Did the coach provide you any personal feedback? Did you have any highlights? Did you have areas of improvement?

....
....
....
....
....
....

TRAINING

Date: / / **Start time** :

End time :

Skills Completed
Write down the skills you worked on and developed during your training sessions

....
....
....
....

Skills to improve
Write down areas that you can improve on for your next training session

....
....
....
....

Coach & Team Focus
Write down if your coach or team has a skill or game focus you are working on

....
....

Extra Notes
Do you have additional notes or thoughts you would like to write down?

....
....
....

GAME DAY

Date: /   /   **Start time**   :

Location: ....

Home Game   **Away Game**

Game Details

.... **Vs** ....

Game Result

             Goals   Goals

Our Score   Opposition Score

Coach Feedback

....
....
....

My Performance   Write down how you felt you contributed to the game. Did the coach provide you any personal feedback? Did you have any highlights? Did you have areas of improvement?

....
....
....
....
....

TRAINING

Date: / /   **Start time** :

End time :

Skills Completed
Write down the skills you worked on and developed during your training sessions

....
....
....
....

Skills to improve
Write down areas that you can improve on for your next training session

....
....
....
....

Coach & Team Focus
Write down if your coach or team has a skill or game focus you are working on

....
....

Extra Notes
Do you have additional notes or thoughts you would like to write down?

....
....
....

GAME DAY

Date: / /   **Start time** :

Location: ....

Home Game ⬤   **Away Game** ⬤

Game Details

.... **Vs** ....

Game Result

　　　　　Goals　　　　　　　　　　　Goals

Our Score　　　　　Opposition Score

Coach Feedback

....
....
....

My Performance — Write down how you felt you contributed to the game. Did the coach provide you any personal feedback? Did you have any highlights? Did you have areas of improvement?

....
....
....
....
....

TRAINING

Date: / /   **Start time** :

End time :

Skills Completed   Write down the skills you worked on and developed during your training sessions

....
....
....
....

Skills to improve   Write down areas that you can improve on for your next training session

....
....
....
....

Coach & Team Focus   Write down if your coach or team has a skill or game focus you are working on

....
....

Extra Notes   Do you have additional notes or thoughts you would like to write down?

....
....
....

GAME DAY

Date: / /   **Start time**   :

Location: ....

Home Game　　　**Away Game**

Game Details

.... **Vs** ....

Game Result

　　　　　Goals　　　　　　　　　　　Goals

Our Score　　　　　Opposition Score

Coach Feedback

....
....
....

My Performance   Write down how you felt you contributed to the game. Did the coach provide you any personal feedback? Did you have any highlights? Did you have areas of improvement?

....
....
....
....
....

TRAINING

Date: / /   **Start time** :

End time :

Skills Completed
Write down the skills you worked on and developed during your training sessions

....
....
....
....

Skills to improve
Write down areas that you can improve on for your next training session

....
....
....
....

Coach & Team Focus
Write down if your coach or team has a skill or game focus you are working on

....
....

Extra Notes
Do you have additional notes or thoughts you would like to write down?

....
....
....

GAME DAY

Date: /   /   **Start time**   :

Location: ....

Home Game   **Away Game**

Game Details

.... **Vs** ....

Game Result

        Goals   Goals

Our Score   Opposition Score

Coach Feedback

....
....
....

My Performance

Write down how you felt you contributed to the game. Did the coach provide you any personal feedback? Did you have any highlights? Did you have areas of improvement?

....
....
....
....
....
....

TRAINING

Date: / / **Start time** :

End time :

Skills Completed   Write down the skills you worked on and developed during your training sessions

....
....
....
....

Skills to improve   Write down areas that you can improve on for your next training session

....
....
....
....

Coach & Team Focus   Write down if your coach or team has a skill or game focus you are working on

....
....

Extra Notes   Do you have additional notes or thoughts you would like to write down?

....
....
....

GAME DAY

Date: / /   **Start time**   :

Location: ....

Home Game ○   **Away Game** ○

Game Details

.... **Vs** ....

Game Result

　　　　　　Goals　　　　　　　　　　　Goals

Our Score　　　　　　Opposition Score

Coach Feedback

....
....
....

My Performance   Write down how you felt you contributed to the game. Did the coach provide you any personal feedback? Did you have any highlights? Did you have areas of improvement?

....
....
....
....
....

TRAINING

Date: / / **Start time** :

End time :

Skills Completed
Write down the skills you worked on and developed during your training sessions

....
....
....
....

Skills to improve
Write down areas that you can improve on for your next training session

....
....
....
....

Coach & Team Focus
Write down if your coach or team has a skill or game focus you are working on

....
....

Extra Notes
Do you have additional notes or thoughts you would like to write down?

....
....
....

GAME DAY

Date: /   /   **Start time**   :

Location: ....

Home Game ◯   **Away Game** ◯

Game Details

.... **Vs** ....

Game Result

            Goals   Goals

Our Score   Opposition Score

Coach Feedback

....
....
....

My Performance   Write down how you felt you contributed to the game. Did the coach provide you any personal feedback? Did you have any highlights? Did you have areas of improvement?

....
....
....
....
....

TRAINING

Date: / /

Start time :

End time :

Skills Completed
Write down the skills you worked on and developed during your training sessions

....
....
....
....

Skills to improve
Write down areas that you can improve on for your next training session

....
....
....
....

Coach & Team Focus
Write down if your coach or team has a skill or game focus you are working on

....
....

Extra Notes
Do you have additional notes or thoughts you would like to write down?

....
....
....

GAME DAY

Date: /   /   **Start time**   :

Location: ....

Home Game   **Away Game**

Game Details

.... **Vs** ....

Game Result

        Goals   Goals

Our Score   Opposition Score

Coach Feedback

....
....
....

My Performance   Write down how you felt you contributed to the game. Did the coach provide you any personal feedback? Did you have any highlights? Did you have areas of improvement?

....
....
....
....
....

TRAINING

Date: / /   **Start time** :

End time :

Skills Completed
Write down the skills you worked on and developed during your training sessions

....

....

....

....

Skills to improve
Write down areas that you can improve on for your next training session

....

....

....

....

Coach & Team Focus
Write down if your coach or team has a skill or game focus you are working on

....

....

Extra Notes
Do you have additional notes or thoughts you would like to write down?

....

....

....

GAME DAY

Date: / /   **Start time** :

Location: ....

Home Game ⚪   **Away Game** ⚪

Game Details

.... **Vs** ....

Game Result

    Goals   Goals

Our Score   Opposition Score

Coach Feedback

....
....
....

My Performance   Write down how you felt you contributed to the game. Did the coach provide you any personal feedback? Did you have any highlights? Did you have areas of improvement?

....
....
....
....
....

TRAINING

Date: / /   **Start time** :

End time :

Skills Completed Write down the skills you worked on and developed during your training sessions

....
....
....
....

Skills to improve Write down areas that you can improve on for your next training session

....
....
....
....

Coach & Team Focus Write down if your coach or team has a skill or game focus you are working on

....
....

Extra Notes Do you have additional notes or thoughts you would like to write down?

....
....
....

GAME DAY

Date: / / **Start time** :

Location: ....

Home Game ⬤ **Away Game** ⬤

Game Details

.... **Vs** ....

Game Result

         Goals   Goals

Our Score   Opposition Score

Coach Feedback

....
....
....

My Performance   Write down how you felt you contributed to the game. Did the coach provide you any personal feedback? Did you have any highlights? Did you have areas of improvement?

....
....
....
....
....

TRAINING

Date: / /

Start time :

End time :

Skills Completed
Write down the skills you worked on and developed during your training sessions

....
....
....
....

Skills to improve
Write down areas that you can improve on for your next training session

....
....
....
....

Coach & Team Focus
Write down if your coach or team has a skill or game focus you are working on

....
....

Extra Notes
Do you have additional notes or thoughts you would like to write down?

....
....
....

GAME DAY

Date: / /   **Start time** :

Location: ....

Home Game ○   **Away Game** ○

Game Details

.... **Vs** ....

Game Result

　　　　Goals　　　　　　　　　　　　Goals

Our Score　　　　　　Opposition Score

Coach Feedback

....
....
....

My Performance Write down how you felt you contributed to the game. Did the coach provide you any personal feedback? Did you have any highlights? Did you have areas of improvement?

....
....
....
....
....
....

TRAINING

Date: / / **Start time** :

End time :

Skills Completed — Write down the skills you worked on and developed during your training sessions

....
....
....
....

Skills to improve — Write down areas that you can improve on for your next training session

....
....
....
....

Coach & Team Focus — Write down if your coach or team has a skill or game focus you are working on

....
....

Extra Notes — Do you have additional notes or thoughts you would like to write down?

....
....
....

GAME DAY

Date: / /   **Start time** :

Location: ....

Home Game ⬤   **Away Game** ⬤

Game Details

.... **Vs** ....

Game Result

        Goals   Goals

Our Score   Opposition Score

Coach Feedback

....
....
....

My Performance

Write down how you felt you contributed to the game. Did the coach provide you any personal feedback? Did you have any highlights? Did you have areas of improvement?

....
....
....
....
....

My Hockey Journal

-Hockey-

03

SEASON NOTES

NOTES

NOTES

NOTES

NOTES

My Hockey Journal

-Hockey-

04
Autographs & Photos

Autographs & Photo's

Autographs & Photo's

Autographs & Photo's

Autographs & Photo's

HOCKEY
Journal

The Life Graduate
PUBLISHING GROUP

-Hockey-

www.ingramcontent.com/pod-product-compliance
Lightning Source LLC
LaVergne TN
LVHW060213080526
838202LV00052B/4270